ASHFORD
VISUAL RECOLLECTIONS

STEVE R. SALTER

For Mum, Dad and James

Dedicated to
Richard Charles Filmer
26/9/1946–5/5/2017
An absolute gentleman and lovely man with an
exemplary knowledge on his specialist subjects
and a wonderful sense of humour.
Thank you so much Richard for your support, encouragement, kindness and
generosity over the years – and for being a wonderful friend!

In memory of
Peter William Goodwin
23/12/1935–27/5/2017
A genuinely lovely man and absolute gem,
someone who could instantly lift your spirits
and make you happy with his joyful disposition. A kind and thoughtful man
who would go out of his way to help. Thanks Pete for the memories!

Copyright © 2017 Steve R. Salter
First Edition 2017
Published by Destinworld Publishing Ltd.
www.destinworld.com
ISBN 978-1-9997175-4-4
Printed in EU by Pulsio Print
British Library Cataloguing-in-Publication Data
A catalogue record for this book is available from the British Library.

CONTENTS

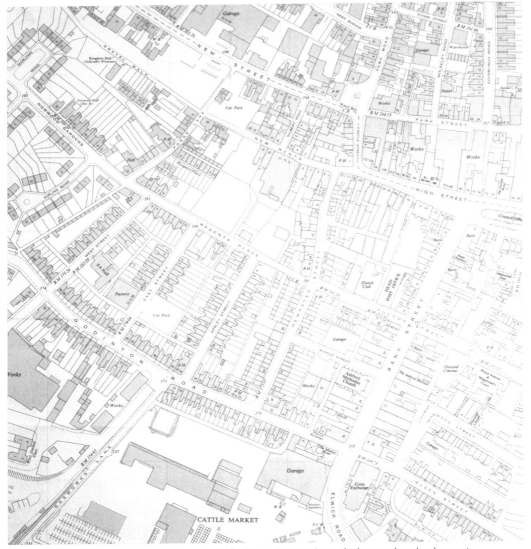

1958 Ordnance Survey Map showing Ashford Town Centre prior to the large scale redevelopments.
© Crown Copyright
Reproduced from 1958 Ordnance Survey Map with kind permission.

INTRODUCTION

For decades, time stood still for the town of Ashford. Even the coming of the railway in 1842 didn't intrude into what was for many years an old-fashioned town with many traditional qualities. Ashford stood for decades without mass development and up until the mid-1960s, to many, the town centre felt more like a country village than a market and railway town with potential to expand. It was smart and unspoilt, the independent trader ruled the roost and everybody knew everybody – well that's how it felt!

The town has always had a knack for survival. Even during the dark days of the Second World War in suffering much heartache at the hands of the enemy, it bounced back. It was always a popular market town with something for everyone. There were no ridiculous road schemes or out-of-town shopping developments to suppress trade on the High Street. Although traditional, Ashford was a town that people loved and visitors flocked to.

It was in the 1960s that fortunes were to change for Ashford. Decisions regarding infrastructure came from central government, while those who owned property or land were keen to maximise their bank balances. Land changed hands and previously developed brownfield sites were transacted. It was all about the money and few cared about the consequences unless they were directly affected by the plans. Towns up and down the country were subjected to controversial planning decisions, and Ashford was one of them.

One cringes when looking back at photographs of old Ashford, in particular at some of our losses when it comes to heritage. The destruction of the many of the town's beautiful old buildings was widespread, and for many it's still a bitter pill to swallow all these years later. Radically different approaches to heritage preservation implemented by Ashford's neighbouring local authorities served to dilute confidence in the town's own administration and ultimately led to feelings that criticisms needed to be made, or that someone should be held accountable.

Over the last 60 years, Ashford has earned a reputation for being a bit of an architectural wilderness, with what can only be described as an often nondescript mismatch of modern versus old. This is also the case in a number of nearby towns, whereas others use a more sensitive approach, ultimately preserving the rich character of the established surroundings. Those who moved to the town around 60 years ago perhaps didn't foresee that the Ashford they found desirable enough to move to then would alter so much – but what about those of us who have lived here all our lives and through the changes?

Town planning is a highly complex and often controversial field of expertise, but how many planners of the 1960s and '70s had a conscience when pulling down countless elements and features that national historic bodies embrace today? How many in authority felt for those whose business or residence was destroyed in the name of progress, uprooted after generations in the same place? To this day, we would love to know how planners came to agree such a controversial set of plans for Ashford. While a town obviously needs to grow, to move forward and to prosper, where these plans are concerned must have been scope for a bit of fine tuning. There must have been a more sympathetic approach that could have been applied.

Old Ashford was certainly a town to be proud of, a town that more or less had everything, so why allow it to be changed so much? There are, of course, things that needed to happen for the town to progress and expand, but there are also things that should never have been allowed to happen – such as abandoning the town's strong values. Ashford had a vast selection of independent traders which were the envy of neighbouring towns. Today, although still in existence, a mixture of high overheads and a difficult economic climate drive away the independent trader like never before. There are barely any longstanding traders surviving in the town today.

Ashford: Visual Recollections follows on from my hugely popular book, *Ashford: A Rare Insight* – as well as my other earlier titles – and provides a comprehensive portfolio of unseen and rare images depicting many of the losses and changes to our market town. This new book also focuses on some of the aspects of the expanding town, many of the images illustrating a number of the more unforgivable changes that have been endured over the years. It provides an unrivalled sentimental photographic record of Ashford in days gone by that will undoubtedly provoke mixed emotions about life in the town during such changeable times.

Steve R. Salter
October 2017

CHAPTER ONE

....

CHERISHED MEMORIES

Elwick Road, 27 March 1971. A nostalgic view depicting one of the original and key routes into town from the railway station and Romney Marsh. The entrance to the famous Ashford Market, which opened in July 1856, can be seen on the left, adjacent to the footpath leading over the railway line by means of a footbridge to Victoria Park. The detached property Elwick Villa can be seen to the right, next to the Elwick Works of motor and tractor engineer Stanhay. This view was to alter dramatically in the years that followed, mainly owing to the construction of the Ringway. *(Edwin Bartlett)*

Victoria Road, 1971. A rare view taken from the south side of the railway line. Here we see the cattle and livestock sheds running parallel to the South-Eastern railway line, historically convenient when carriages were used to transport the livestock. The former and long-lost West station can be seen (centre left) and can be identified as the building with numerous chimney stacks. *(Edwin Bartlett)*

Ashford Cattle Market, Elwick Road, 1969. A rare gem depicting a traditional market scene at the long-standing site. This photograph dates from before the days of the vast changes that saw the market's footprint reduced for both the Ringway and latterly the High-Speed rail link, by which time the market had relocated to a new site in Sevington where it still thrives to this day. The top of Elwick Road and foot of Bank Street can be seen in the background with the premises of Stanhay and the one-time Methodist Church. Note the old traditional wooden hurdles dividing the sheep for sale. *(Edwin Bartlett)*

Ashford Cattle Market, Elwick Road, 1972. A substantial amount of alterations have been made since the previous photograph was taken and can be clearly seen in this view while the market was closed. The new Ringway had been built by this time, and involved acquiring some of the market site and removing the old ornate entrance gates and brick gatehouse. One can also see that demolition is progressing on the opposite side of the road. The Elwick Works of Stanhay are in the process of being demolished, while the new Tufton Shopping Centre can be seen under construction in the background. Utilised by the local council years back, and a replacement for the much-missed Corn Exchange, Trafalgar House can be seen on the right. *(Edwin Bartlett)*

Ashford Market, Elwick Road, 1972. A memorable view showing the market during one of its other uses as a market for clothes, food and other wares. Even carpets and rugs are being sold in this view. *(Edwin Bartlett)*

Ashford Market, Elwick Road, 1972. Further to the left, this view shows many of the old market buildings and later cattle pens which were extensively upgraded by the late 1970s. The modernisation of the Elwick Road site saw many of the older buildings demolished as a result, although several were subsequently retained. *(Edwin Bartlett)*

Elwick Road, 2 May 1972. A rare view showing the doomed auction rooms fronting Elwick Road. The building was replaced by an office block which for many years served partly as the town's register office, among other uses. At the time of writing, the complex has been converted for residential use. *(Edwin Bartlett)*

Elwick Road, 2 May 1972. Many old Ashfordians will remember the one-time Elwick Auction Rooms, which were located behind the former Corn Exchange and alongside the lane that runs from Queen Street to Elwick Road. They were the auction rooms of Burrows & Co., and were subsequently demolished in late 1972. *(Edwin Bartlett)*

Elwick Road junction with Godinton Road and Bank Street, 1972. A splendid picture showing one of the town's many long-lost hostelries. The Market Hotel can be seen here at the corner of Godinton Road in its Ind Coope brewery livery. The neighbouring premises of Stanhay awaits the bulldozer, but the Market Hotel (latterly renamed the Wig and Gavel) survived another 21 years before it was prematurely demolished. The site wasn't redeveloped until 2005 when the County Square shopping development was extended. *(Edwin Bartlett)*

Godinton Road junction with Hempsted Street, 9 April 1972. One of many of the town's streets obliterated by redevelopment. This view, showing Godinton Road, sees residential terraces surrounding another of the town's much-missed locals. The Invicta at the corner of Hempsted Street (right) also survived until the early 1990s when, together with the last remaining terraces in Hempsted Street, it was demolished. The terraces pictured to the left and behind the Invicta were bulldozed in the months after this picture was taken. *(Edwin Bartlett)*

Godinton Road junction with Apsley Street, 2 November 1971. Nowadays, the dying licensed trade sees many hostelries closed, converted or even demolished. One would think that their long histories (many of the pubs pre-date other old buildings in our town), would make them candidates for preservation whether they continue as licensed premises or not. However, the planners and developers have other opinions which do not always secure the futures of these ancient properties. The Elephant and Castle pictured here is one of the lucky survivors. It is no longer operates as a public house, but is now a Nepalese bar and eatery. *(Edwin Bartlett)*

Godinton Road, 2 November 1971. This rare picture illustrates Godinton Road at the start of the 1970s, during such time that the street became extensively segmented between Elwick Road and West Street. There was no urgency nor apparent need to demolish many of the residential properties and businesses so early, but many were bulldozed for the Ringway and subsequent land development where housing once stood. The houses from left to centre still survive today, but the terraces (pictured right) with their colourful gardens were demolished for the road scheme which necessitated the widening of West Street. *(Edwin Bartlett)*

New Street, 13 June 1971. More recently owned by Faversham brewer Shepherd Neame, the British Volunteer public house, seen here in its Whitbread Mackeson guise, is one of the town's recently closed venues. Locals were alarmed when the new owners put in an application to demolish the former coaching inn and replace it with residential units. After a local outcry, the developer withdrew the plans and converted the old Volunteer instead. The retention of the façade and sympathetic treatment of the original architectural design has paid dividends and ultimately satisfied those who fought for it to be saved. The two residential properties at nos 52 and 54, together with the neighbouring premises, Violet Perkins, tobacconist, at no. 50, were demolished in the early 1980s so that the neighbouring Caffyn's Garage could extend its forecourt. *(Edwin Bartlett)*

New Street, 1972. The 1970s was the era for a drab olive colour scheme, but I am unsure what possessed brewer Whitbread to paint the outside of the pub that colour! *(Edwin Bartlett)*

Barrow Hill, 2 May 1973. Today, Barrow Hill is largely a conservation area where many Grade II Listed buildings of national significance exist. Until recently, the former Prince of Orange (behind the camera) was listed, but following a suspicious blaze, the owner succeeded in getting the property de-listed and the former public house which dates to 1680 faces an uncertain future. There are plans to replace the buildings, parts of which are well over 300 years old, with a block of apartments. Incidentally the blighted property at no. 111 just misses the conservation area. The long-lost former Engineer public house can be seen on the immediate left. Until its demolition in the early 1980s, it stood near the Prince of Orange. *(Edwin Bartlett)*

New Street, 7 June 1970. Caffyn's Garage (previously Hayward's) has been sentimentally captured in this view which also shows local people undertaking the local Rotary Club's 25-mile walk. The British Volunteer public house can be seen in the distance together with Violet Perkins, tobacconist, at no. 50 and the one-time premises of Ozonic Mineral Water at nos 46–48 next door. The former Caffyn's site was redeveloped in the late 1990s. *(Edwin Bartlett)*

St George's Square, 6 July 1972. A splendid view showing the Mark IV First World War tank no. 245, which was presented to the town in August 1919 in recognition of the people's generous response to the National War Savings Appeal. The Prince of Wales public house can be seen on the left, with the New China City Restaurant (now demolished) pictured right. A protective cover was built for the tank in 1987. *(Edwin Bartlett)*

St George's Square, 1972. This view shows the tank pictured from Castle Street where it joins New Street, with the junction of Park Road on the right. *(Edwin Bartlett)*

Wolseley Road, 26 June 1971. A personal favourite, this lovely picture shows the Park Hotel which once stood at no. 21 Wolseley Road at its junction with Stone Street. Sandwiched between a closely grouped residential area, the Park was one of many Courage houses in the town during this time. A stone's throw from other public houses, beer lovers were never short of choice. Sadly, this once-popular haunt was yet another hostelry on the developers' hit list. It was demolished in 1972 for the impending Ringway. *(Edwin Bartlett)*

Forge Lane, 26 March 1971. This wonderful colour view shows another of the town's many lost hostelries. It was in 1972 that the Fremlin's-owned British Flag was demolished to make way for the new Ringway. The Flag, one of the town's smallest locals, is seen here in all its finery together with Record Corner at the top of New Rents (far right) and the scrap business of C.J. Anderson (centre right). Prospect Place just creeps into view on the right. *(Edwin Bartlett)*

Park Road, 1972. One of several largely residential streets to barely exist today is Park Road. This view, looking towards Albert Road, shows the junction of Kent Avenue on the left with Park Road Post Office at its corner and Stone Street further along on the right. The chosen route of Ringway between New Street and Somerset Road carves its way through this street today. *(Edwin Bartlett)*

Tufton Street junction with Bank Street, July 1972. A hugely nostalgic view which gives an unobstructed view of Tufton Street looking towards Hempsted Street. The Wellington Hotel just creeps into view (centre left) adjacent to the one-way sign, with the Coach & Horses public house at the corner of Hempsted Street and Regents Place in the distance (centre right). Many will remember the existence of the Elwick Club next door to the post office in the days before the Tufton Centre was built. Upon the demolition of their premises illustrated here, the club moved to a new purpose-built site in Church Road. Trice's florist can be seen on the immediate left. *(Edwin Bartlett)*

Tufton Street, 1972. These ornate almshouses were built on land given by George Elwick Jemmett, Esq., with a legacy of James Wall, Esq. in the early 1800s. They were located opposite the Elwick Club and behind the Wellington Hotel. The beautiful properties were to fall foul of the developer and were demolished to make way for the Tufton Shopping Centre in late 1972. *(Edwin Bartlett)*

Tufton Street, 1972. A very rare and largely forgotten view taken in Tufton Street outside the post office, looking towards Hempsted Street and further on to Regents Place and Apsley Street. The long-lost Wellington Hotel sits at the corner of Hempsted Street opposite the neighbouring Coach & Horses. Both hostelries were owned by Maidstone brewer Fremlin's who are famous for their elephant motif. The warehouses of H. Carey, wholesale fruit and vegetable merchant, can be picked out in the distance (beyond the telephone box) at the corner of Apsley Street and Regents Place. The terraced houses beyond the latter are all that remain in this view – everything else illustrated was sacrificed for the shopping centre development. *(Edwin Bartlett)*

Regents Place junction with Hempsted Street and Tufton Street, July 1972. This obscure gem, taken early one summer evening, gives us a rare look at Tufton Street from its junction with Hempsted Street and Regents Place. Taken outside the Coach & Horses public house (left), it shows the Wellington Hotel (right) and the Elwick Club further along on the left, adjacent to the post office. The Swan public house can be seen in the distance in the black and white timbered building on the left of the street. Tufton Street and its junction with Bank Street falls just beyond the red motor vehicle. Everything in the foreground up to the point of the post office sadly does not exist today. County Square shopping centre now covers the site. *(Edwin Bartlett)*

Hempsted Street, July 1972. A sad view taken further to the right of the previous photograph, illustrating the impending and ongoing demolition in preparation for the shopping development. The Wellington disappeared together with the greater portion of Hempsted Street in the months that followed. The rear of the Bank Street Methodist Church can be seen in the background (right). Incidentally, the Congregational Church was also demolished in 1972, but its spire can be identified (far left) here. The church stood at the junction of Tufton Street and Church Road. *(Edwin Bartlett)*

Hempsted Street, 2 June 1972. A splendid view showing the upper section of Hempsted Street just months before the bulldozers moved in. The former Wesleyan Chapel, utilised for many years by W.H. Gibbs for storage, can be seen on the right adjacent to wasteland where a row of ancient cottages had once stood. It was a case of 'keeping up appearances' for many property owners who are visibly continuing to maintain their doomed properties – but not for others. The weatherboarded premises of Dann's second-hand furnisher (far left) is looking rather sorry for itself. Streets like Hempsted Street are often subject to preservation orders nowadays. *(Edwin Bartlett)*

Hempsted Street, 18 November 1971. The Coach & Horses public house was one of the last buildings to be demolished for the shopping centre development. Images exist which show the progression of the new development surrounding the former local. Many customers will remember that the pub's final licensees were Edward ('Ted') and Lily Cager. This view looks towards the upper section of Hempsted Street where it joins New Rents. *(Edwin Bartlett)*

Church Road, 1967. In years past, Ashford had many more beautiful buildings certainly worthy of preservation and retention. One is infuriated that the removal and ultimate destruction of buildings such as these villas in Church Road and latterly the Congregational Church at the corner, was permitted by the planners of yesteryear. This is not careful planning; it is extreme sacrilege. These properties and church were replaced largely by today's crumbling police station and recently defunct magistrates court. Rumour has it that there is possibly no intention of replacing the police station which opened in 1969, and that the site will be sold for redevelopment. *(Edwin Bartlett)*

Hythe Road, 27 April 1971. Happily, these residences and business premises still exist at the foot of Hythe Road and will hopefully never be considered for redevelopment or demolition. Residents will recall the shops illustrated such as F.T. Egan, general stores, at no. 106 with Hanson's fish shop at no. 104 and W.J. Thorn, butcher, at no. 102. The premises of A.J. Chalmers Ltd, wholesale grocery and confectioner, can be seen further to the right at nos 98–100. None of the businesses mentioned are still trading today. *(Edwin Bartlett)*

Hythe Road, 27 April 1971. Many of us forget how this section of Hythe Road looked before the alterations of the last 40 or so years were implemented. The former mill of H.S. Pledge at East Hill is still easily recognisable today, together with the school buildings of Ashford School behind the trees (centre) and the former tax office (far right), but the most notable difference is the road layout. In April 1971, traffic travelling into town from Hythe Road still used East Hill. Also, East Hill was one-way and traffic leaving the town towards Hythe Road would use Mace Lane. It is apparent that the Ringway had yet to be completed and the other side of Mace Lane was not yet built. Note the wide expanse of grass where the road now exists. The former premises of wool merchant Gregory and Prentis can be seen (centre) at the corner of East Hill. Comprehensive demolition has been carried to everything on the left of this picture. *(Edwin Bartlett)*

Hythe Road, 27 April 1971. This particularly rare view illustrates the terraced cottages that once stood at the foot of Hythe Road, adjacent to the River Stour and East Hill Mill. It is believed that one of the properties was used as a shop many years back and one former resident told me that these cottages were prone to flooding. Today there is no evidence of the cottages ever having existed on the site. *(Edwin Bartlett)*

Hythe Road, 27 April 1971. A closer look at the cottages that once stood in Hythe Road beside the River Stour and adjacent to East Hill Mill. *(Edwin Bartlett)*

Hythe Road, 1972. Reputable monumental mason; F.H. Russell operated from the bottom of Hythe Road for generations. Working with marble, granite and stone, they proudly advertised 'British worked memorials a speciality'. Their more recent and final showroom and works are seen here with the entrance to Henwood Industrial Estate on the left. The long-standing business closed in the 1980s and an office development was constructed on the site in the early 1990s. *(Edwin Bartlett)*

Mace Lane junction with East Hill, 27 April 1971. Looking up the hill towards Somerset Road, this view shows Mace Lane where it leaves the town towards Hythe Road and passes through part of the one-time site where Gregory and Prentis, wool merchants, once operated. One of their main buildings still survives in this view, albeit boarded up. This and the remaining house next door were demolished upon the construction of the town-bound carriageway of Mace Lane. The Queen's Head public house which once stood to the left of the house, was demolished in March 1968. *(Edwin Bartlett)*

East Hill, 27 April 1971. Another view showing the former premises of Gregory and Prentis alongside the houses that remained after earlier demolition took place. The Star public house can be seen beyond the trees in the background (centre) and the Provender Mill and mill house at East Hill Mill can be seen on the left. It is these two elements that were destroyed by an arson attack on 16 May 1974. *(Edwin Bartlett)*

East Hill, 27 April 1971. Still a popular local today, the Star public house can be seen on the left at a time when the former general store of Christina Judge is still being utilised for an unknown purpose. Its doorway is blocked by the sign 'Star Car Park: Grills'. The former shop was demolished in the mid-1970s to create more space for the car park. The one-time entrance to Anchor Cottages can be identified adjacent to the lamp-post on the left between two houses belonging to Ashford School: Northside (nearest the Star) and Bridge House the other side of the entrance also on the left. Ashford School's main buildings are situated beyond the substantial wall on the right. *(Edwin Bartlett)*

North Street junction with Somerset Road, 22 March 1971. A wonderful and very rare picture of the long-lost Somerset Arms public house that once stood in North Street at the corner of Somerset Road. The much-loved regular haunt was one of the many public houses that stood at the main entrance routes into town – this one sitting on the main A28 Ashford–Canterbury road, so the likelihood of the Somerset having been a coaching inn is strong. The attractive Courage house, together with the adjacent row of houses and business premises of Ashford Bakeries/Alfred Joint Stock Bakery, were demolished for the Ringway. The premises of the Tunbridge Wells Equitable Friendly Society (also demolished) can be seen on the extreme right of the picture. *(Edwin Bartlett)*

Somerset Road, 1971. The entrance to the public bar of the Somerset Arms at the side of the building in Somerset Road. Chambers Garage can be seen creeping into view on the extreme left. *(Edwin Bartlett)*

North Street, 30 April 1971. At the time of its eventual demolition in 1972, the Lord Roberts public house in North Street was said to have been the oldest hostelry in the town. The Courage-owned business, which had previously been the Red Lyon, is seen here in its last few months of trading. There was a public outcry when the popular local was demolished to make way for a new service road extending Park Street. The two adjacent premises illustrated –W.H. Gibbs, house furnisher and Denne's the seed merchant – still survive today as restaurants; Pizza Express and the Paper Duck respectively. *(Edwin Bartlett)*

Somerset Road, 1972. A splendid view of the Trumpeter Inn at the bottom of Somerset Road where it meets Wellesley Road. The Trumpeter's neighbour for many years were the offices of the Ashford Conservative Association (pictured right), and had once been the Cruden House School. Previously the Wellesley Inn, no. 49 ceased to be a public house in the late 1980s and remained near derelict for several years. In the late 1990s, however, popular pizza takeaway chain Domino's converted the premises into their Ashford branch. *(Edwin Bartlett)*

Wellesley Road, 1961. A very rare view showing the driveway that served the rear of many of the businesses and properties in the Lower High Street, such as the County Hotel and Westminster Bank. County Components at nos 13a–15 Wellesley Road can be seen on the left. *(Steve Salter Archive)*

Wellesley Road junction with East Hill and Station Road, 13 June 1971. Still spoken of by many who remember it, the handsome Duke of Marlborough public house is seen here in its dominant position at the top of East Hill. It destruction for the Ringway in 1972 was a crime, and many were extremely critical of the sacrilegious attitude of planners during which time it seemed the whole town was being pulled apart. The Refuge next door, another of Ashford School's premises, survived the bulldozer. *(Edwin Bartlett)*

Station Road, 29 March 1971. Work has commenced in earnest to demolish some of the buildings in Station Road for road widening at this point. Anything in the way of the new Ringway was sadly sacrificed. Those premises on the left (pictured) were also some of those lost to the new road. From left to right, C.I. Epps and Sons Ltd, builders and monumental masons at no. 24, Star Taxis at no. 20, Barnardo's (previously Universal Photo Service) at no. 18, Betty's ladies' hairdresser at no. 16 and F. Bucknell, confectioner at no. 14. The Baptist Church, albeit remodelled today (centre) and Pearl Assurance House (now Northdown House) next door (centre), plus the premises of Pricerite supermarket (centre), are all that survive today. *(Edwin Bartlett)*

Station Road, 1971. The once-familiar premises of C.I. Epps, builders and monumental masons, are pictured before their subsequent expansion and relocation to Bridge Road, Cobbs Wood Industrial Estate. Epps, established in 1841, sadly ceased trading at the end of 2015 after 174 years in the town. *(Edwin Bartlett)*

Dover Place, 2 May 1972. In the early 1970s, Dover Place not only underwent alterations to build a proper road, but it was also around the time that construction commenced on International House. The office complex was built on the site of the former Lion Brewery. The premises of the Ministry of Labour and National Service can be seen on the left, together with the workshops of Crouch's Garage to the rear. The business of Eastes and Loud, seedsmen, can be seen adjacent to the telegraph pole on the right, and the one-time Fremlin's off-licence is on the immediate right. *(Edwin Bartlett)*

Victoria Road, 19 April 1968. Rarely seen from the rear in photographs, this view shows the Victoria Flour Mills of H.S. Pledge in Victoria Road. The mill, which was built in 1890 and stood on the edge of the railway line between the coast and London, was one of two that operated in the town centre at that time. Pledge's other mill, built in 1901, was situated at East Hill and operated until 1972. On 7 September 1984, an arson attack all but destroyed Victoria Mills, which not only necessitated total demolition of the ancient building, but also saw Pledge's departure from the town. *(Edwin Bartlett)*

Beaver Road, 19 April 1968. Relatively recently departed in consideration of the other mass redevelopment in and around the town, this view illustrates the Victoria Hotel at the corner of Beaver Road and Victoria Road, together with the Butcher's Hotel and Restaurant (left). In its latter days, the Victoria ceased to be a hotel and was finally demolished together with the Butcher's Hotel in the late 1990s. At the time of going to press, supermarket chain Aldi have plans to build a new supermarket on this now-derelict site. *(Edwin Bartlett)*

CHAPTER TWO

OLD-FASHIONED BUT FAVOURED

Lower High Street, 1974. A memorable view depicting the Lower High Street when independent traders were still plentiful in the town, among the national chain stores. Headley, grocer, dominates the picture at no. 46, together with Headley Brothers next door at no. 44 which was the home of the family's retail and wholesale stationery department, sub-post office and fancy goods. In 1976, no. 46 was demolished and the upper elevation built in the same style. The individual Headley Brothers departments were largely amalgamated into the new larger shop, by which time Headley's grocery business had moved to Bridge Road. No. 46 is now the home of a McDonalds restaurant. The Chocolate Box at no. 48 is the only business trading (albeit with different owners) in this location today. *(Richard Filmer Archive)*

Lower High Street, 1960. The green unspoilt fields beyond the Lower High Street are evident in this rare view taken from the church tower of St Mary the Virgin. Developments such as Charter House, the Ringway, the tax office and Henwood had yet to be built at this time, and there is a notable gap in the distance between the landmark water tower at the Batchelors Foods site and the factory itself, confirming that the neighbouring Proprietary Perfumes factory and offices had yet to be built. *(Richard Filmer)*

Lower High Street, 1960. Further to the right, it is interesting to note suburban Willesborough in its pre-development days. Foxglove Estate had yet to be built, too. The Lower High Street (left) joins East Hill from Station Road and Wellesley Road (centre), with East Hill Mill dominating the bottom of East Hill where it joins Hythe Road. In the days before the Ashford bypass, traffic travelling between the coast and London had little choice but to utilise the streets through the heart of Ashford, some very narrow, such as East Hill. *(Richard Filmer)*

Lower High Street, 1960. A splendid view showing the Lower High Street at Christmas time in 1960 and looking towards Middle Row. At the time this section was still open to two-way traffic. The area has largely been pedestrianised nowadays thus spoiling this traditional street scene. The situation isn't helped by the treacherous cobbles and paving installed in recent times. *(Richard Filmer)*

Lower High Street, 1962. This wonderful view taken at a Royal Marines parade, really gives a feel for the town as it used to be, and before the immense changes in the years that followed. The popular department store of Ashford Co-operative Society can be seen centrally at nos 24–28. The ornate building replaced the society's earlier premises which were destroyed by fire in 1926. Next door, at no. 22, a new store for Pricerite Wear N' Ware can be seen in its final stages of construction, replacing the former premises of Lee's bedding centre, while clearly discernible to the right, the businesses of Marshall Fashions; ladieswear, and the counter service store of J. Sainsbury can be seen at nos 16 and 18 respectively. The major supermarket chain moved to new premises on the site of the former Saracen's Head Hotel at no. 56 High Street in 1968. *(Richard Filmer)*

Lower High Street, 1970. At one period, no. 31 (pictured centre) was the home of Fendall's, wine merchant, who latterly moved to no. 9 North Street. It was also a public house many years back called the Ounces Head. Here we can see that the occupants at that time are several. Scott and Kendon's estate agent office takes the larger portion of the building, which is also known as St John's Chambers. The once-successful business operated from part of the ground floor and upper floors in this picture, while Betabake occupy the centre. Long separated from the main building, the left-hand side of no. 31 is occupied by The Wine Market, an off-licence (latterly Victoria Wine). The unforgettable and much-missed Gizzi restaurant can be seen further to the left at no. 29. *(Richard Filmer)*

Lower High Street, 1962. This sentimental and atmospheric view illustrates the wide expanse of High Street where it tapers off into Middle Row. It shows both Midland Bank at no. 39 and G.V. Crump, grocer, at no. 41 (left), with Kennington Laundry & Dry Cleaners at no. 45, Baldwin's Travel Service and Tudor Rose, drapers at nos 47 and 49 respectively (further along on the left). Nos 45, 47 and 49 were rebuilt after the departure of Stevenson's, fishmonger and greengrocer, a few years earlier. Scotts Dyers can be seen in the timbered building at no. 13 Middle Row (centre) with Sercombe's, gentlemen's outfitters at no. 12. The unusual chimney sign of the Man of Kent public house can be seen in the background above Scotts. *(Reflections/Weavers 1962)*

Lower High Street looking towards Middle Row, 1962. Another view taken from outside no. 46, this time showing the narrowing High Street adjacent to Middle Row with St Mary the Virgin in the background. It is here that many of the town's oldest buildings are found. *(Kentish Express)*

Middle Row, 1962. A splendid view showing the premises of Scotts Dyers, today better known as popular sandwich and pastry shop The Carvery, alongside the central section of Middle Row which was historically known as the 'Butchers Shambles'. Rabson's toy shop can be seen to the left at no. 55 High Street, with Sercombe's on the right, humorously advertising 'GO FOR Y-FRONT UNDERWEAR!' on the outside wall. *(Steve Salter Archive)*

Lower High Street looking towards Middle Row, 1970. Eight years later, the beautiful timbered and characterful building at no. 13 Middle Row (now Flinns Cleaners) has been rendered over – an unthinkable act today. Also, the drapery business of Tudor Rose at no. 49 High Street has become Babyland & Junior Wear. Scores of youngsters of a certain age (including me), will remember the mechanical weighing scales outside the door. *(Studio Photocraft)*

High Street (Middle), 1970. The quaint and picturesque area which separates the Upper and Lower High Street is seen here, illustrating many long-lost independent trades, in particularly focusing on the immediate left of the picture. Closest to the camera is Knott's shoe shop at no. 51, which disappeared in the late 1970s. Knott's had previously operated from premises in Station Road which were redeveloped for Pearl Assurance House. Next door, Rabson's watchmaker and jeweller traded into the early 1990s from no. 53, while the family's toy shop business could be found next door at no. 55, the latter barely trading into the 1980s. *(Studio Photocraft)*

High Street (Middle)/Kings Parade, 1970. Taken from the High Street looking back towards the point that the previous picture was taken, this splendid view again shows trade names of the past such as Dixon's ironmongers (centre) at no. 7 Middle Row, which had ceased trading by the end of the 1970s. Also prominent in this view is Bodsham's Farm Shop at no. 4, which also disappeared around the same time. Kent shoe retailer Walter and Son (pictured right), was a more recent departure from the town in around 2007. *(Studio Photocraft)*

Elwick Road, 1970. Many Ashfordians were angry when plans were passed to demolish the Corn Exchange at the top of Elwick Road. The destruction of the popular multi-use venue made way for new offices for national insurer Commercial Union (pictured right). More recently people have spoken out about how beneficial the Corn Exchange would have been to the town in modern times. The junction of Godinton Road can be seen further along on the left, with Queen Street opposite on the right. *(Studio Photocraft)*

Bank Street, 1965. The incline of Bank Street is not always apparent in reality, but this rare view gives the impression that the main throughfare to the town centre is on quite a slope. At the time of this photograph the street was open to two-way traffic, but is absolutely deserted. It is interesting to note some of the businesses trading here, which include Doughty's tobacconist at no. 37, W. Thompson, commercial printers and stationers, at no. 35b, the Singer sewing machine shop at no. 35a, W.A. Oxford, optician, at no. 33a and Curry's Ltd, cycle, radio and television shop at no. 31, to name but a few. *(Studio Photocraft)*

Tufton Street junction with Bank Street, 1965. Today, this section of Tufton Street remains largely unaltered, except for the trades which have all but faded into the past. In the distance, the once-popular Swan public house can be seen while still under Courage ownership (right), with funeral director: F.C. Wood at no. 21. Next door (centre right), Stanhay's used car centre and garage workshops can be seen, together with Brown's electrical contractor at no. 25, D.T. and E. Knight, watchmaker and jeweller at no. 27 and Ashford Sanitary Laundry at nos 29–31. The premises of G. Herbert, pawnbroker and jeweller, can be seen on the left at the corner of Tufton Street and Bank Street. *(Studio Photocraft)*

Upper High Street, 1970. In the days before being completely pedestrianised, the upper section of the High Street was open to traffic and looked like this. Prior to July 1957, when the bypass opened, motor vehicles and lorries had no other choice but to use the heart of the town. Even after the bypass opened, at peak times gridlocked streets were a regular occurrence, so planners set about designing a road to relieve the town's traffic flow issues. The infamous Ringway was criticised on many points, but one of the main gripes was that it was built too close to the town's heart, thus strangling the centre itself. Upon its creation, many streets were stopped up and others, such as this, were pedestrianised. This section was completed by 1977. *(Studio Photocraft)*

Upper High Street, 1970. A fantastic view showing the Upper High Street before many of the controversial changes were under way. It's hard to decipher the reasons for this bad planning and the removal of such attractive sections of the town and its heritage. It is here that the High Street entrance to County Square Shopping Centre now stands. The menswear department of Lewis and Hyland occupies the tall building (centre) at no. 93, with Arthur Prince's betting shop at no. 95, Dewhurst butcher at no. 95 a and house furnisher W.H. Gibbs at nos 97–9. J. Price, jeweller and watchmaker, just creeps into view at no. 101. Incidentally, the beautiful clock is now located outside NatWest Bank in the Lower High Street. It was refurbished after laying undiscovered for years. *(Studio Photocraft)*

New Rents, 1972. Many Ashfordians of a certain age will have fond memories of the well-known department store Lewis and Hyland, which once dominated the south side of New Rents. The business was started by George Alexander Lewis in 1834, and latterly Frederick Hyland joined Lewis as business partner. The firm, which also opened stores in Folkestone, Hastings, Tenterden and even Pluckley, grew from strength to strength, but in Ashford all was about to change in the 1970s when the landmark store was earmarked for redevelopment. The store was demolished in 1976 after the business moved into the new Tufton Centre. By 1980, Lewis and Hyland had ceased to trade. *(Steve Salter Archive)*

New Street, 1957. A rare view illustrating a post-war New Street and showing the absent features of the street as a direct result of the war. Haywards Garage can be seen on the right, together with the British Volunteer public house further along on the right. There had previously been several houses on the left, but these fell victim to the intense wartime bombing in the vicinity, which also hit the nearby garage and Snashall's Bakery, resulting in the loss of numerous lives. The terraces in the distance (centre) were demolished in 1973 for a new roundabout and the road was subsequently widened, which necessitated tearing down the remainder of the houses on the left up to the point of the Prince Albert and Prince of Orange public house at nos 109 and 111 New Street. *(Steve Salter Archive)*

New Street, 1961. Since the mid-1960s, the site on the immediate left has been home to the St John's Ambulance Brigade at their purpose-built headquarters, Furley Hall. The house next door was for many years used as the St Joseph's Convent School but has now been converted back into a private residence. A fine example of the work of Edwin Pugin (son of the eminent architect Augustus Pugin), the Roman Catholic Church of St Teresa of Avila next door was not recognised as an architectural gem or a building of merit, and was subsequently demolished in 1993 to be replaced by a building without any external merit whatsoever. *(Bryan Sales)*

New Street, 1961. A lovely period view showing a busy New Street at its junction with Magazine Road (left), prior to the intense demolition the street suffered in the preceding years. The houses on the right with the unconventional dormers and those at the junction (left), were demolished for a new roundabout. The houses and businesses further down on the left, along with the Prince Albert and Prince of Orange (centre right), escaped that round of destruction. The latter, however, is currently the subject of a demolition proposal following a deliberate fire that edged the properties (which were partly listed) towards a de-listing order. *(Richard Filmer)*

St Georges Square, 1960. This rare view shows the town's First World War tank in the days before its purpose-built protective cover was erected. Park Road can be seen in the background. The curved building (far left) was for many years the New China City Restaurant. Folkestone Glass Works can be seen on the right. *(Richard Filmer)*

Park Street junction with Park Road and Castle Street, 1950. Today this once-populated residential and business artery is no longer a through road; it ceased to be so upon the construction of Park Mall Shopping Centre in 1985. As well as housing its own properties, Park Street has for many years served as a 'service road' for the rear of the Upper High Street. There are very few properties of any vintage left in this section of Park Street. One of them, no. 11 Park Street, the home of Stafford Perkins, chartered surveyors, has just been extensively refurbished. Its owner, Richard Stafford, has been applauded by many (including myself) for his attention to detail in bringing the building back to how it looked many years ago. *(Steve Salter Archive)*

North Street, 1972. Weeks before their demolition for the new Ringway, the dwellings and businesses at nos 34–44 North Street are pictured, with the junction of Somerset Road on the immediate left. Upon closer inspection, Charter House can be seen in the early days of its construction. *(Lambert Weston)*

North Street, 1969. In 1968, supermarket giant J. Sainsbury opened their first self-service store at the corner of High Street and North Street. The development, which was constructed by local firm C.I. Epps, was built on the site of the Saracen's Head Hotel, whose frontage dominated the perimeter of the street. Upon the arrival of Sainsbury's, this previously claustrophobic section of the street appears wider. Forsyth the furrier's premises can be seen on the immediate left at no. 4 with much-missed milliners and costumiers Ashley Russell Ltd. at no. 2 (far left). The Mocha Bar can be seen in the distance below the church tower at no. 1 Middle Row, with Doughty's tobacconist and the vacant Bartlett and Best premises at nos 2 and 2a respectively (centre). *(Studio Photocraft)*

Somerset Road, 1961. These charming terraces in Somerset Road were also in the line of fire where redevelopment was concerned. Scores of residents were displaced all over the town when compulsory purchase notices were served. These houses were not only levelled for the Ringway, but for Charter House too! *(Lambert Weston)*

Wellesley Road, 1970. At the start of the 1970s, the top end of Wellesley Road between the High Street and Somerset Road had remained unaltered for generations, but by December of the following year, work had started on the new Charter House building. In the months that followed, the terraces seen here adjacent to the trees in Somerset Road and nos 11–15 Wellesley Road on the left (occupied by Emetco Ltd, electric meters), were bulldozed for the new building. In 2017, work commenced on building apartments at the corner of Somerset Road and Wellesley Road where these residential dwellings once stood, as well as further along Somerset Road, as part of phase two of The Panorama – the new name for Charter House. *(Lambert Weston)*

Station Road, 1972. Today, the Royal Mail sorting office and the car park adjacent to restaurant The Everest Inn largely cover the site of these once beautiful and substantial houses, some of which had been converted for business use on the ground floor. The road was widened as part of the Ringway project that was completed by 1974. Plans necessitated the demolition of these properties up to the point of the former Ashford Working Men's Club. Some property owners escaped by the skin of their teeth by losing a section of their garden or part of their driveway, but others lost their properties under the compulsory purchase laws. *(Steve Salter Archive)*

Station Road, 1972. In the late 1990s, Crouch's Garage in Station Road closed after generations at their site adjacent to the Ashford Working Men's Club and at the corner of Dover Place. At the time of this picture, they are selling National fuel and specialising in Hillman, Humber and Commer motor vehicles, although prior to their demise at Station Road, they were a Ford dealership. The office block behind was occupied at one time by Kent County Council's buildings department, as well as Dearle and Henderson, quantity surveyors, and South Kent Group Training Association. The house on the right was for many years the offices of the Ministry of Labour and National Service. After the departure of Crouch's (who moved much of their business to their Willesborough and Kennington sites), and the other businesses in the offices, the buildings became derelict and were demolished in 2006, to be replaced by a council car park. A substantial office development is currently being built on the site. *(Steve Salter Archive)*

Station Road, 1963. A splendid view showing Crouch's Garage nine years earlier. The 1930s frontage together with its 'sunshine' bay windows were remodelled in the 1970s for a more modern appearance. Note the beautiful Vauxhall Cresta and Hillman motor cars parked outside. *(Sylvia Marsh/Bryan Sales)*

Elwick Road, 6 June 1972. A rare view showing a much narrower Elwick Road. Today it appears much wider, even at the section which has been given over to Shared Space. The former South Kent College of Technology can be seen on the right, together with Crompton House where Kent County Council's children's department, register office and youth employment office were once located. Next door, Swanton House was for many years used for the County Council's social services department. The overflow car park to the nearby Ashford station can be seen on the left. Many residents will remember The Cottage, just visible on the left, where Grace Oglesby ran her fruit and flower business years ago. *(Edwin Bartlett)*

CHAPTER THREE

DIARY OF DESTRUCTION

Park Road, Ashford, 1972. Work has commenced in earnest in Park Road to dismantle these terraced properties and recover their readily reusable materials. They had stood for generations but were in the path of the new Ringway, as were many other properties in the town centre. An incredible sadness surrounded families upon their departure of these charming residences, particularly for those who were part of several generations of the same family that had lived at the property in question. *(Edwin Bartlett)*

Park Road, Ashford, 1972. Seeing street after street looking like this was certainly commonplace around the town at this time. Scores of private residences were laid bare once the demolition contractors commenced their operations to clear the site. Here we can see wallpaper-covered chimney breasts exposed for all to see. In this picture, looking towards Blue Line Lane and Albert Road, the exposed interior of the house is the demolition line where flank walls were made good with external-faced brickwork. Some properties on the edge of the road scheme that escaped demolition have since been extended by utilising the parcels of land left over where neighbouring houses once stood. *(Edwin Bartlett)*

Park Road, Ashford, 1972. This view, looking from the rubble of Kent Avenue, illustrates the houses from the earlier picture, minus their roof trusses and coverings. The chimney pots of other doomed houses beyond can be seen in the background. How many former residents drive along this road today and reminisce about their former homes, realising they are driving through what was once their front room, kitchen or dining room? *(Edwin Bartlett)*

Park Road, Ashford, 1972. A dramatic view taken alongside a partly demolished terrace, illustrating Kent Avenue and Sturges Road and a field of rubble from the houses which has been utilised as a base for the new road. On closer inspection, a kerb line for the new road can be picked out adjacent to Sturges Road and in the foreground. *(Edwin Bartlett)*

Kent Avenue/Sturges Road, 1972. Substantial sections of Kent Avenue have disappeared already in this view, which shows Sturges Road to the right and the rear of Caffyn's Garage site in the background. Much of the demolition around this time was undertaken by the demolition contractors Fuggle and Sheridan, whose bulldozer can be seen on the right. Incidentally, the site where the mound of rubble lies (centre left), had been the pre-war premises of local baker Snashall's and was one of the notable bomb sites in the town during the Second World War where residents' lives were lost. *(Edwin Bartlett)*

Forge Lane/New Street, 1972. Surviving residential dwellings and businesses sit among this view which resembles a war zone. It shows a realigned Forge Lane in the foreground and New Street passing centrally left to right of the picture. Caffyn's Garage can be seen on the immediate left, with Kent Avenue (centre left) and Sturges Road (centre). Several businesses were cleared at this point in New Street to accommodate the new road. *(Edwin Bartlett)*

Wolseley Road, 1972. The once popular and attractive Park Hotel is seen here at the road's corner with Stone Street during demolition for the Ringway. Although it sat at the edge of the new road, it was still deemed necessary to flatten it. It is interesting to note that at the time of demolishing the former Courage-owned hostelry, it would appear that a fire broke out. Evidence can be seen at the removed bay window (centre), and upper floor. *(Edwin Bartlett)*

Wolseley Road, 1972. Another particularly rare view, showing that demolition has already taken place on the terraces next door to the former Park Hotel (centre) and on the immediate left. This view of Wolseley Road shows Stone Street (centre right) with Saracen's Garage (centre left) and Park Street in the background. *(Edwin Bartlett)*

North Street junction with Somerset Road, 1972. Further along the path of the Ringway, a sub-base and kerb line has been laid where dwellings once stood. On closer inspection, the garden wall of those large houses that once faced Somerset Road can be picked out. The Courage-owned Somerset Arms public house can be seen (centre) in what was probably its final few weeks of trading. The neighbouring one-time premises of Ashford Bakeries Ltd (left), was already being taken apart. Another blighted business premises was that of the Tunbridge Wells Equitable Friendly Society (right). That too fell foul of the development plans, together with the adjoining houses. Chambers Garage can be seen on the left at a time before the garage was extended and redeveloped in the 1980s. The business's long association with Shell fuel and lubricants ended a few years back when the garage was rebranded for Applegreen fuel. *(Edwin Bartlett)*

North Street, 1972. A rare view taken outside the business of the Tunbridge Wells Equitable Friendly Society at no. 44 North Street shows the progressing Ringway project alongside Blue Line Lane and Chambers Garage. The garden wall behind the road sign belonged to the large houses that had faced Somerset Road at nos 30 and 33. You would have to stand in the middle of the busy Ringway to photograph this area today. *(Edwin Bartlett)*

North Street, 1972. One of many sad sights around the town during the early 1970s was the demolition of the historic Lord Roberts public house in North Street, which, at the time of its demolition, was reputed to be the oldest in the town. Its destruction, together with the premises of John Hogbin, estate agent, (left) at no. 5, was to make way for a new service road linking Wellesley Road and Park Street. Looking back, many locals question the motives and decisions of the planning authority during those turbulent times. *(Edwin Bartlett)*

New Street, 1972. Demolition was deemed necessary at New Street where it met Magazine Road as part of the Ringway scheme. Here, the ancient residences and business premises of tobacconist Mr C.J. Leaver (centre), are being prepared for demolition, as are those on the immediate right. New Street had suffered bombing raids in 1943, so the demolition of these additional properties came as unwelcome news. Two survivors of the scheme, the Prince Albert public house (centre) together with the Prince of Orange next door (out of view) are currently subject of thoughtless proposals to demolish both former hostelries which are on the edge of a conservation area, and replace them with a multi storey block of flats. *(Edwin Bartlett)*

New Street junction with Magazine Road, 1972. Today, any health and safety inspector would have kittens looking at this pre-regulation view of nos 113–141 being dismantled. Nowadays, netted scaffolding and a suitable hoarding would be required to protect passing pedestrians and vehicles from harm. *(Edwin Bartlett)*

New Street, 1972. A sad view showing the vacant premises of Leaver's tobacconist and confectioner at no. 127 New Street, shortly before its demolition. The once-familiar vending machines have been removed in this view. The Leavers continued to trade for several more years at their other shops in Bank Street and latterly Middle Row, where Anne, daughter-in-law of Mr Leaver (senior), served until the business was sold. *(Edwin Bartlett)*

New Street, 1972. Looking towards the town centre, empty dwellings await demolition. The Prince Albert public house can be seen further along on the right. *(Edwin Bartlett)*

New Street, 1972. Opposite, work was already under way to demolish the houses between the Magazine Road junction (pictured left) and the premises of David Easton, TV and radio repairer at no. 74 New Street. At the time of writing (2017), though still trading, David is considering hanging up his soldering iron; he is one of the town's longest-serving independent traders. *(Edwin Bartlett)*

Magazine Road, 1972. St Mary the Virgin Church can be seen in the distance, peeping above the rooftops of these former dwellings being demolished in New Street. This picture is taken at the rear of the terraces in New Street. *(Edwin Bartlett)*

Magazine Road, 1965. A fantastically rare action shot showing the water tower in Magazine Road being demolished to the rear of the Roman Catholic Church of St Teresa of Avila and adjacent to the Ashford Urban District Council Highways yard. Note the largely forgotten allotments to the rear, between the yard and the one-time cricket ground. *(Richard Filmer)*

Hempsted Street, 1972. Demolition had already taken place on the lower section of Hempsted Street a few years earlier – between the Invicta public house and Regents Place and running parallel with Apsley Street. This street, together with the west side of Apsley Street, a section of Middle Street and Tufton Street, was compulsorily purchased for the Hempsted Street shopping development (latterly called the Tufton Centre) as early as 1963. This view, taken at the street's junction with Tufton Street, illustrates that demolition is already underway on some of the neighbouring properties of the Coach & Horses public house. No. 14, the premises of G.A. Lee, turf accountant, had totally gone at this point. New Rents can be seen in the background. *(Edwin Bartlett)*

Hempsted Street, 1972. If you lived in one of these Ashford town centre properties during the 1970s, there's a chance that many more people than you would have liked would have seen your bedroom wallpaper – as this picture of demolition in the lower section of Hempsted Street shows! A council car park replaces some of the terraces which have already gone (left). It was still difficult for many who lived in streets such as this one, seeing their homes and old stomping grounds being pulled apart. The junction of Middle Street can be seen beyond the Volkswagen camper van (right), with the junction of Tufton Street further along where the Coach & Horses public house and Wellington Hotel can be seen still standing. *(Edwin Bartlett)*

Hempsted Street, 1972. Today, such bold acts of destruction – where ancient buildings like these are concerned – are largely a thing of the past, but at the time of writing, planners have still not completely learned their lesson. Despite their powers, many local authorities buckle under the slightest pressure rather than fight to retain their heritage. This view shows the premises of G.A. Lee at no. 14 Hempsted Street, surrounded by what would be perfect candidates for preservation today – and should have been then. The popular and long-forgotten business of Dann's second-hand furnisher can be seen in the red-fronted and weatherboarded building at no. 8, together with P. Fowle, boot and shoe repairer next door at no. 4 (both centre right). *(Edwin Bartlett)*

Hempsted Street, 1972. The remaining section of no. 14 Hempsted Street, showing the telephone exchange (left) and the rear of the Lewis and Hyland department store in New Rents (right). *(Edwin Bartlett)*

Hempsted Street, 1972. A splendid but sad view showing this once-familiar crossroads in Hempsted Street. With a public house on each corner, one can imagine the amount of activity outside during trading hours. The Wesleyan Chapel, which was being used here as storage for furnisher W.H. Gibbs, can be seen in the tall building (centre). The cottages next door and at the junction with Tufton Street have already been pulled down. *(Edwin Bartlett)*

Hempsted Street, 1972. Weeks later, demolition of the Wellington Hotel seemed imminent as the neighbouring residences have all but disappeared. The Elwick Club and almshouses in neighbouring Tufton Street were also demolished for the project. *(Edwin Bartlett)*

Hempsted Street, 1972. Trade has ceased at the Coach & Horses pictured at the corner of Hempsted Street and Regents Place. Until its closure, the pub was owned by Maidstone brewer Fremlin's, but the removal of the sign at the corner has revealed a previous owner – 'Coach and Horses, Flint's Canterbury Ales'. The telephone exchange can be seen in the background. *(Edwin Bartlett)*

Tufton Street, 1972. The historic and beautifully ornate almshouses in Tufton Street during their demolition for the new shopping centre development. The building on the left still survives today and has for many years been the home of a Wimpy restaurant. *(Edwin Bartlett)*

Tufton Street, 1972. In this sad view taken outside the sub-post office, cars park on the former Elwick Club site and work has commenced to finally demolish the Coach & Horses. The houses pictured far left in Apsley Street, still survive today. *(Edwin Bartlett)*

Hempsted Street, 1972. Cellars are all that remain where the residences and businesses in Hempsted Street once stood. This picture shows the old Elwick Club shortly before its demolition, next door to the sub-post office in Tufton Street that still survives today. The almshouses, which stood opposite, have already been demolished at the time of this photograph. The ragstone cellar nearest the camera would have been the cellar to TV and radio repairer David Easton's premises at no. 51, which had stood at the junction with Middle Street. *(Edwin Bartlett)*

New Rents, 1976. While it escaped the main demolition of neighbouring Hempsted Street for the new shopping development, this view shows the demolition of long-lost department store Lewis and Hyland in New Rents. The long-established firm had taken two new units in the new Tufton Shopping Centre development by this time, and this picture shows some old signage which was uncovered during demolition work. The Tufton Centre can be seen in the background and through where the department store once stood. Note the ornate window bars of the shop frontage. *(Richard Filmer)*

Middle Street, 1972. An early evening view taken in the early 1970s showing the redundant and one-time business premises of Ashford Motors (left), which was also sacrificed for the Tufton Centre development. The Methodist Church situated in Bank Street can be seen on the right, together with the street itself (centre). One of the shopping centre's service yards now occupies the former garage site. *(Edwin Bartlett)*

Hempsted Street, 1972. This view, taken near to the junction with Godinton Road, shows the side and rear of the former premises of the Kent Sweet Works in Middle Street. Ashford Motors can be seen on the extreme left. The works were also demolished for the shopping development. *(Edwin Bartlett)*

Elwick Road, 2 June 1972. The Elwick Auction Rooms of one-time Ashford auctioneer Burrows & Co., are seen here being torn down to make way for the new office block which for many years contained the register office and the offices of the Kent Probation Service. In recent times, the building has been converted into residential apartments. *(Edwin Bartlett)*

Elwick Road, 1972. A memorable view illustrating the long-lost business and premises of Stanhay's at the top Elwick Road. The agricultural engineering firm had made its mark on the town and was one of Ashford's key employers for many years. At the time of this picture, Stanhay's had moved their premises to Godinton Way as these premises and Elwick Villa (centre left) were set for demolition, albeit prematurely. The site wasn't utilised for redevelopment until 2005 and remained a car park until such time. To the right, popular photographic dealer Colourscope Cameras, run by the kindly Bob Jarvis, can be seen. Their later premises were situated in the Tufton Centre and were sold out to Jessops when Mr Jarvis retired. None of the trades mentioned exist in the town today. *(Edwin Bartlett)*

Elwick Road, 1972. A small section of the familiar frontage still exists in this view showing the former Market Hotel (latterly the Wig and Gavel public house) to the right. Ashford Market can be seen in the background. *(Edwin Bartlett)*

Elwick Road, 1972. Clouds of dust rise into the air as workmen tear down Elwick Villa which stood next to Stanhay's main showroom. The terraces in Godinton Road – long demolished now – can be seen in the background (right). *(Edwin Bartlett)*

Elwick Road, 1972. An East Kent double-decker bus sweeps into Bank Street from Elwick Road. Here we see the demolition site adjacent to the Market Hotel (left) with Trafalgar House and the tool shop of Parkers of Canterbury (right). *(Edwin Bartlett)*

Elwick Road, 1972. The crater left by the demolition of Stanhay's has been back-filled in this view, which also reveals part of a sign on the uncovered gable end of the Market Hotel (though unfortunately it is not possible to discern any telling detail). In 2005, work commenced to extend the neighbouring County Square Shopping Centre. This work involved inserting piles around the site's perimeter and at the time I notified the site agents of contractor Laing O'Rourke that Stanhay's used to sell fuel from the pavement's edge many years back, and that there was a possibility that the fuel tanks were still in situ. My prediction was right – three massive fuel tanks had to be retrieved from the ground when the piling rig hit one. Bank Street can be seen in the background. *(Edwin Bartlett)*

Church Road, 1972. The tower of the Congregational Church which once stood at the corner of Church Road and Tufton Street is pictured here clad in scaffolding. One would like to think that the church was being renovated or repaired, but unfortunately, the former landmark was another victim of what appears to have been a 1972 demolition spree. A few years later, the site became the home of a new magistrates court for the town. *(Edwin Bartlett)*

Somerset Road junction with Wellesley Road, 11 November 1971. In December 1971, work started on the new headquarters for mining finance giant Charter Consolidated. The new triple-winged complex was named Charter House and was constructed at the same time as the Ringway. A month earlier, terraces in Somerset Road were being demolished to make way for road widening near to Charter's site. Several decades later, developers are putting residences back where these houses once stood. The Trumpeter Inn can be seen on the right. *(Edwin Bartlett)*

Station Road, 28 April 1971. In nearby Station Road, demolition contractors work to strip the former premises of Hoskins tobacconist of its Kent pegged roof tiles. The windows of this and the adjoining premises have already been removed and internal doors were reused to create a makeshift hoarding to protect passers-by. Today the bustling Ringway carves its way through this area. Many people using the road nowadays would not have a clue that it once looked so different before planners were ruthless with the town. *(Edwin Bartlett)*

Station Road, 27 April 1971. A bus conductor crosses the road where mass demolition is taking over. The County Market stores were the next building to face the bulldozers, its roof already removed by the look of the timbers piled on the roof. Pearl Assurance House (left) had recently been completed here. The retail units had yet to be let. *(Edwin Bartlett)*

Station Road, 11 June 1971. Well-known businesses at that period, such as Hoskins, tobacconist, County Market Stores and Tiffany's café, have all gone and the attractive Duke of Marlborough public house is next in line. Nowadays, with ever-increasing traffic levels, the town would have struggled if the roads had been left as they were, but surely a little more thought should have been given to alternatives that do not bring demolition at every corner? One-time supermarket chain Pricerite's premises, which were built in 1968, can be seen on the left. *(Edwin Bartlett)*

Station Road, 13 June 1971. A Walls ice-cream sign is all that remains outside of where the former premises of Hoskins once stood. It is apparent that demolition hadn't long finished judging by the piles of timber joists and beams left on site. Sadly, work to demolish the Duke of Marlborough (left) was only days away. East Hill can be seen at the centre left of this view. *(Edwin Bartlett)*

East Hill, 25 June 1971. A closer view of the East Hill elevation shows that some of the windows and doors had been removed while workmen stripped out the Duke of Marlborough's interior. *(Edwin Bartlett)*

Station Road, 25 June 1971. Although the Duke of Marlborough was Watney's-branded, the former public house still displayed a clock on its curved exterior in the name of Reid's Stout. Up until 1958, the brewery was known as Watney, Combe Reid & Co. Ltd. In this view, the clock had been removed prior to the demolition of the premises. I wonder where that clock is today? *(Edwin Bartlett)*

East Hill, 30 June 1971. Days later, the beautiful roundel roof has been removed, as well as the main roof and rear of the former hostelry. The building on right, belonging to Ashford School, still survives today. *(Edwin Bartlett)*

East Hill, 3 July 1971. The beautiful building which once was the Duke of Marlborough is nothing but a pile of rubble in this sad view. *(Edwin Bartlett)*

Lower High Street junction with Station Road and East Hill, 6 July 1971. The rubble left over from the demolition of the Duke of Marlborough has been cleared, revealing the outline of the former public house against the neighbouring building and the remaining interior walls of the former Watney's house. *(Edwin Bartlett)*

Wellesley Road, 6 July 1971. Upon closer inspection, one of the Duke's fireplaces sits among the scarred walls of the once-popular watering hole. *(Edwin Bartlett)*

Station Road, 20 March 1972. This view, taken at the top of today's adopted road of Tannery Lane, shows no. 83 Station Road –once the home of the Ministry of Pensions and National Insurance – being torn down for road widening. The neighbouring business premises of Whittingham's, wool merchants (right), at no. 85, together with all the properties up to the Ashford Working Men's Club building, were also demolished. *(Edwin Bartlett)*

Beaver Road, 1972. Those with an interest in heritage preservation can and will never understand how planners could have allowed the destruction and removal of grandeur such as this. The beautiful house pictured here was called Harlech House and was for many years the home of Ashford practitioner Dr R. Denny. It is seen here during its demolition for a new petrol station opposite the one-time business premises of automotive engineers John Wilment. The group of business premises alongside it, including Kennett's newsagents, the Butcher's Hotel and the Victoria Hotel, were not demolished until 1998. *(Edwin Bartlett)*

Beaver Road, 1972. A rare view showing the old Trumpet Bridge over the River Stour in Beaver Road and near to the open-air swimming baths. John Wilment, automotive engineers, can be seen on the right, while demolition is ongoing at Harlech House further along on the left. The ground surrounding the house on the river's edge is being worked to accommodate the new garage. *(Edwin Bartlett)*

Hythe Road, June 1974. Nowadays, this section of Hythe Road has a roundabout leading into both Henwood and Mill Court. The latter was once the site of the Ashford Underwear Company, and latterly Energen/Rank Hovis McDougall. Here, the houses which once stood on the left, are being demolished for a new entrance to the Energen site. The gutted shell of East Hill Mill can be seen on the left. The vacant former business premises of flour miller H.S. Pledge had been severely damaged by fire a month earlier. *(Edwin Bartlett)*

CHAPTER FOUR

SUBURBIA: DISTANT DAYS

Newtown Road, 1965. Here we see the well-known landmark clock tower and entrance to the once-bustling Ashford Railway Works. All the buildings illustrated, including the two towers, still exist to this day, but other buildings on the site have either been demolished or lie derelict. Many have often had dreams of a full-scale railway museum like the splendid one at York on the former works site, but developers and the local authorities haven't been tempted enough. *(Bryan Sales)*

Beaver Road, 1965. A lovely picture from mid-1960s suburbia, showing three of the street's long-forgotten traders. Co-operative Laundry and Dry Cleaning stands at no. 57, while next door is Ealham's, newsagent and tobacconist, at no. 59, advertising Lyons Maid Ice-Cream and Woodbine cigarettes on their shop frontage. The chemist of A.P. Hartman can be seen at no. 61. *(Bryan Sales)*

Beaver Road, 1965. There was always a bit of competition for the independent trader in past times, more so than today. This view shows the neighbouring business of F.G. Bell, tobacconist and confectioner, at no. 53, together with its wool and fancy goods shop next door (left) at no. 51. Some of these former shop premises have since been turned into self-contained flats. *(Bryan Sales)*

Christchurch Road, 1965. Still identifiable as a former shop today, this nostalgic view shows the one-time Christchurch Stores at no. 47. It has since been converted into a private residence. *(Bryan Sales)*

Beaver Road, 1965. A splendid picture showing the long-lost business of W. Jones & Sons, cycle agent and filling station, at no. 105 Beaver Road and on the corner of Whitfield Road. Again, these former business premises have been converted for living accommodation. *(Bryan Sales)*

Kingsnorth Road, 1965. Sadler's Stores, grocers, provisions, tobacco and off-licence, can be seen in this rare view at no. 26 Kingsnorth Road and near to the junction with Beaver Lane. In recent years no. 26 has been a hairdressing salon. *(Bryan Sales)*

Beaver Road, 1965. Streets such as Beaver Road were never short of stores such as tobacconists, confectioners, grocers or butchers. This picture shows the long-forgotten Beaver Road Stores at no. 139, advertising Heinz 57 baked beans and soups in the window. *(Bryan Sales)*

Kingsnorth Road, 1965. A stone's throw away from Sadler's, the greengrocery business of R.J. Hargreaves operated for many years from no. 46. More recently, the premises were the home of automotive dealer Beaver Batteries. *(Bryan Sales)*

Kingsnorth Road, 1972. Long-term residents and book lovers will remember the former South Ashford branch of Kent County Library at the Kingsford Memorial Hall, seen here in its derelict state in 1972. This and the house next door were subsequently demolished and replaced by a group of modern terraced dwellings. *(Edwin Bartlett)*

Kingsnorth Road junction with St Stephens Walk, 1972. Another view taken at the junction, showing the Kingsford Memorial Hall and house next door, which were both demolished. *(Edwin Bartlett)*

Kingsnorth Road, 1965. Another of Kingsnorth Road's many resident independent traders was the business of A.J. Gardner, post office and general store, seen here at no. 63 with its convenient forecourt outside. Not a 4×4 nor a badly parked car in sight! Today, tempers flare outside convenience stores around the town. With many more cars on the road, there never seems to be enough room to park. *(Bryan Sales)*

Kingsnorth Road, 1965. The ever-popular Bungalow Stores at the very top of Kingsnorth Road at no. 212. At the time of writing, this convenience store is one of the longest-surviving in the street, albeit under different ownership. *(Bryan Sales)*

Mead Road junction with Gladstone Road, South Willesborough, 1965. In times past, the corner shop ruled the roost over the national chain store, and many nearby residents were reliant on their existence. Not everybody had a car, so shops such as this were a lifeline for many. This picture shows the business of A. & O. Wakefield, newsagent, tobacconist and post office at no. 63 Gladstone Road, at the corner with Mead Road. *(Bryan Sales)*

Cudworth Road, South Willesborough, 1965. This *Open All Hours*-style shop is the general store of F.C. Down at no. 57 Cudworth Road. Nowadays, parents are rightly reluctant to leave a child or pram outside a shop, but this picture hails from an era when things were quieter and life was lived at a much slower pace. Who is the young boy standing outside the door? *(Bryan Sales)*

Hythe Road, Ashford, 1965. More recently, no. 79 Hythe Road has been better known as Raj's newsagent, post office and convenience store, but here the premises at the corner of Star Road were occupied by D. & E.B. Dobson. In the late 1970s the premises were extended to create a bigger store. The shop still represents a valuable and continued commitment to the local community. *(Bryan Sales)*

Mead Road junction with Gladstone Road, South Willesborough, 1965. Directly opposite Wakefield's, at no. 64 Rayners Stores operated as a stationery, tobacconist and grocery business. *(Bryan Sales)*

Hythe Road, Ashford, 1965. A splendid view illustrating the premises of F.T. Egan, general stores, at no. 106. This was part of a parade of business premises that still survives today, with the exception of one or two that have been turned into flats. The Willesborough branch of Hanson's fish and chip takeaway and restaurant can be seen creeping into view on the right at no. 104. *(Bryan Sales)*

Foxglove Estate, 1970. Obscure to many Ashfordians, this picture shows the parade of shops and businesses on the Foxglove Estate during their early years of trading. In the 1960s it was deemed a luxury to have conveniently located businesses within new housing developments. National supermarket chain Pricerite occupies the larger unit on the left with Golden Pin Curl, hairdressers, and the Wallpaper Showrooms (centre). Linton Farm Shops and the Coin Wash launderette can be seen on the right. *(Bryan Sales)*

Church Road, Willesborough, 1968. Built at the start of the 1960s, this view shows the ever-popular parade of convenient businesses in Church Road near to its junction with Hythe Road. This was primarily built to serve the substantial Highfield Estate behind, an estate that has quadrupled in size over the decades. Very few of the businesses or units (if any) are still under the same ownership or being used for the same trade today. *(Bryan Sales)*

Kennington Road, Willesborough, 1965. The comprehensive production site of Batchelors Foods and neighbouring Proprietary Perfumes (far left) are seen at their Kennington Road base. Batchelors, known today as Premier Foods and still producing many of its famous brands, celebrated its 60th birthday in August 2017. Proprietary Perfumes became Quest International in the 1980s. More recently the facilities and business were taken over by the French firm Givaudan, which was founded as a perfumery company in 1895 in Lyon by Leon and Xavier Givaudan. *(Bryan Sales)*

Kennington Road, Willesborough, 1965. The compounding building at the Proprietary Perfumes site which opened next door to Batchelors in around 1962. *(Bryan Sales)*

Kennington Road, Willesborough, 1967. Until the construction of the William Harvey Hospital at nearby Lacton Green, Willesborough Hospital, particularly its maternity department, was the birthplace of scores of Ashfordians (including myself) who were born pre-1978. Previously a workhouse for the East Ashford Union built in 1835, the medical institution was converted to become apartments when it was sold by the health authority. *(Kentish Express)*

Cemetery Lane, Ashford, 1976. In 1975, local entrepreneur and businessman Terry Burch purchased a beautiful but dilapidated Kent pegged barn at the corner of Cemetery Lane and Canterbury Road with a view to restoring it and opening a garden centre. By April 1976, Terry's ultimate dream had come true and the business was ready to open to the public. Supported by his faithful wife Eunice and his three daughters, Terry's tireless work and expertise took the business from strength to strength and, in 1986, it moved from the barn to a new purpose-built centre across the road where he further expanded the business, making it the top of its league in the South East. In 2016 and upon his long-overdue retirement, he sold the hugely profitable business to Surrey-based garden centre chain Longacres. They not only further developed the business and its premises, but happily also retained the Bybrook Barn name. The familiar sign illustrated stood at this junction for many years. *(Steve Salter Archive)*

Cemetery Lane, Ashford, 1976. A memorable view of the original Bybrook Barn garden centre situated in the historic Kent pegged barn. After Terry Burch moved the business from this location, it wasn't until 1997 that the site and barn were converted into a successful Harvester restaurant. Terry had rescued the Victorian glasshouses (right) from Victoria Park and erected them at the garden centre, even moving them to the new site in 1986. Sadly, the ageing structure was deemed dangerous by the time Longacres demolished it in 2017. *(Steve Salter Archive)*

Cemetery Lane, Ashford, 1976. Despite the site's limitations, business was always brisk and the car park was often full, as illustrated in this view of Bybrook Barn shortly after opening. Here we have a much better view of the glasshouses. *(Steve Salter Archive)*

Canterbury Road, Ashford, 1976. It was in 1971 that this main arterial route and part of the A28 Ashford–Canterbury road was widened between Penlee Point and Cemetery Lane. Prior to the widening, the bottleneck caused regular issues at peak periods. One can imagine traffic queuing from here into the town centre, which didn't have a completed Ringway until 1974. The Courage-owned Bybrook Tavern can be seen on the right in the days before hotel chain Trusthouse Forte purchased the site. The massive tree has long been a feature at the roadside and has survived for many decades. *(Steve Salter Archive)*

Faversham Road, Kennington, 1967. For many decades, there has been a parade of shops between Nettlefield (pictured right) and Burton Road further to the left of the picture. Many Kennington residents will remember some of the long-lost businesses such as W. Atkinson, chemist, Kennington Beauty Salon, Holland's hardware shop and, in this view, the general store and newsagent business of C.G. Carter, which can be seen adjacent to the entrance to the Great Burton Farm housing estate. In the early 1980s Carter's was purchased by Bella Patel and her husband, the very kindly gentleman John, and the business became Saver Newsagents. Bella still runs the popular convenience store today. *(Bryan Sales)*

Faversham Road, Kennington, 1974. Further along Faversham Road, this view shows another parade of businesses at the corner of Park Road. From left to right: Co-operative Food Hall at no. 152, The Store, tobacconist and confectioner at no. 154, Poly-Clean launderette at no. 156, Hair Flair at no. 158 and Osbornes, newsagents, at no. 160 (latterly taken over by Peggy Chapman). The Co-operative food hall moved to a new purpose-built supermarket on the site of the former Colt public house in the early 2000s. The young man on the left is amused by the photographer's presence. His flared jeans and hairstyle certainly date the photograph. *(Steve Salter Archive)*

Faversham Road, Kennington, 1975. The Towers Secondary School is pictured at the top of the Faversham Road. The expertise, vision and professionalism of its founding headmaster, Geoffrey Foster, earned the school many accolades under his tenure, making The Towers one of the top secondary schools in the country. Mr Foster was involved in the school's creation as far back as the planning stage and his innovative and ground-breaking achievements right from the outset set an acknowledged precedent for schools across the country to follow suit. His hard work earned him huge respect from his colleagues. He was awarded a well-deserved OBE for Services to Education upon his retirement in 1985. Geoffrey Foster passed away in 2016 aged 91, just short of the school's 50th birthday. *(Steve Salter Archive)*

Oakfield Road, Kennington, 1960. The Bishop of Dover in the presence of the late Reverend E.B. Lewis, Vicar of Kennington, blesses the new St Mary's Church Hall at the top of Oakfield Road. *(Kentish Express)*

CHAPTER FIVE

EXPANSION EVIDENT EVERYWHERE!

Hythe Road, Willesborough, 10 March 1978. In the late 1970s, plans were unveiled to build a new section of the M20 between Ashford and Folkestone. The project, which was awarded to Dowsett Engineering Construction Ltd, involved converting the old Ashford bypass that had opened in 1957 between Maidstone Road/Warren Lane and The Street, Willesborough, and building the new road through to Folkestone. This was to alleviate the strain on the A20, which was at breaking point. This rare view shows a row of cottages that were earmarked for demolition. They occupied the spot where the London-bound slip road stands today. *(Neville Marsh)*

Lacton Way, Willesborough, 10 March 1978. It is commonly known that homes which stand on the routes of substantial road schemes – such as motorways – might potentially be subject to compulsory purchase orders. These 1930s semi-detached properties in Lacton Way are some that were demolished to make way for the new interchange and link roads at junction 10 of the M20. *(Neville Marsh)*

A20 Ashford bypass, Willesborough, 10 March 1978. A very rare view illustrating the bypass looking towards Lacton Way (right) with the junction of The Street, Willesborough and Kennington Road (centre left). Today, the junction 10 interchange sits behind the houses and the M20 carriageways, carving their way through, make this view impossible to re-create. The Tesco Crooksfoot branch (which sits on the site of the former detached house of the same name) sits beyond the group of trees (centre) in the distance. *(Neville Marsh)*

Hythe Road, Willesborough, 10 March 1978. Further towards the site of the today's M20 junction 10, many will recognise the farm that once stood on the site. Little Lacton Farm, owned by the locally well-known Currah family, is seen here along with some of its farmland. All this area is now sadly buried beneath the motorway. The trees on the left surrounding Crooksfoot still survive today. *(Neville Marsh)*

Hythe Road, Willesborough, 10 March 1978. Another view looking back towards the Highfield housing estate (centre), showing Little Lacton Farm on the left. The soon-to-be-demolished semi-detached houses in Lacton Way (centre right) can be clearly seen, and Hythe Road can also be identified on the right. *(Neville Marsh)*

Hythe Road, Willesborough, 7 March 1978. Today it's impossible to pinpoint this scene looking towards the town. It shows several houses on the opposite side of the road in The Street that were also torn down for the new motorway. The bay-windowed semi-detached house (on the right) remains. *(Neville Marsh)*

Hythe Road, Willesborough, 8 February 1979. Work has commenced to both rip up and widen the 1957 bypass and upgrade it accordingly to motorway standards. This view, looking towards Kennington, shows the Foxglove Estate on the left and the Ashford waste water treatment works (centre right). *(Neville Marsh)*

Hythe Road, Willesborough, 25 February 1979. Demolition has already taken place in Lacton Way at the time of this photograph. It shows the land towards Sevington Church (centre right) before the numerous housing developments were constructed, together with the orbital road at Bad Munstereifel Road. *(Neville Marsh)*

Hythe Road, Willesborough, 25 February 1979. It is easy to forget that, prior to the construction of the M20, this roundabout stood at the very top of Hythe Road – today the position of the London-bound slip road for the motorway. The houses in the background still survive today. *(Neville Marsh)*

Hythe Road, Willesborough, 4 August 1979. The roundabout in the previous view has disappeared here, and a new London-bound slip road is being constructed in place of the roundabout. *(Neville Marsh)*

Hythe Road, Willesborough, 2 September 1979. Little Lacton Farm and it its surrounding land is barely discernible is this view illustrating that work is underway in earnest to transform this part of Willesborough beyond all recognition. Earthmovers have already carved out this part of the route and one of the first interchange bridges can be seen nearing completion in the distance. The footbridge over the motorway and accessible from The Street can also be seen being constructed on the right. The Street, Willesborough, became a no through road here because of the motorway's construction. *(Neville Marsh)*

A20 Ashford bypass, 16 December 1979. Towards the end of December and during the final days of the 1970s, a new bridge over Lees Road is seen being constructed to accommodate the new motorway alongside the existing bypass bridge, some of which has already been removed here. Batchelors and Proprietary Perfumes, together with Kennington, can be seen in the distance. *(Neville Marsh)*

A20 Ashford bypass, 24 August 1980. By the following August, the new coast-bound carriageway has been laid alongside the still-operational bypass (centre left), which has been turned into a contraflow arrangement. *(Neville Marsh)*

Lees Road, 21 December 1980. The coast-bound bridge over Lees Road has been completed here and shuttering has been erected to construct the London-bound bridge. The former Willesborough Hospital can be seen under the bridge in the background. *(Neville Marsh)*

Hythe Road, Willesborough, 18 January 1981. This waterlogged section of the M20 site shows the completed footbridge over to a remaining section of The Street, Willesborough. The houses illustrated here are those that survived the changes and still exist today. The William Harvey Hospital can be seen during its first few years of operation in the background. *(Neville Marsh)*

Hythe Road, Willesborough, 19 January 1981. The path of the original Ashford bypass has been obliterated by the progressing motorway construction. Note that the route of the old road is coned off (centre left). Although it is a hazy day, Charter House can be clearly identified in the distance together with Willesborough Windmill behind the trees (centre). *(Neville Marsh)*

Hythe Road, Willesborough, 19 April 1981. An early view of the incomplete section of the M20 and the junction 10 interchange. Site workers' caravans can be seen on the old bypass next to the slip road (left), while Dowsett's site offices were situated in the grounds of the derelict house named Crooksfoot where Tesco Crooksfoot now stands (centre right). Note the absence of the orbital road/Bad Munstereifel Road on the right. *(Neville Marsh)*

Hythe Road, Willesborough/M20 site, 19 May 1981. Contractors spared this tree, which once stood outside Little Lacton Farm and for many years occupied the coast-bound embankment of the interchange at junction 10. Sadly, the tree was removed a few years later after evasive earthworks disturbed its chances of long-term survival. *(Neville Marsh)*

M20 site, 29 November 1981. Nearing completion, this view shows the motorway near to Crooksfoot. Here we see the finishing touches, such as crash barriers and perimeter fencing, being fitted. Many Dowsett vehicles, including a tanker, are parked on what was to become one of the busiest motorways in the country. *(Neville Marsh)*

M20, 2 May 1982. Not necessarily a thing of beauty, but certainly a product of convenience, this view shows the finally completed and newly opened M20 and junction 10. *(Neville Marsh)*

Edinburgh Road, 24 April 1984. These houses and business premises in Edinburgh Road had been earmarked for redevelopment in the post-Ringway days. Until such time that their removal was required, they fell into heavy dereliction. The site's owners, Charter Consolidated, were even urged by the local authority to tidy up the unsightly area. The buildings eventually made way for an extension to the neighbouring Sainsbury's supermarket and the adjoining Park Mall shopping development. The one-time premises of chiropodist Philip Dormer can be seen adjacent to the Arrow Taxi in the white-fronted house, while a White Elephant charity shop can be seen on the left. *(Neville Marsh)*

Edinburgh Road, 24 April 1984. At this time, significant demolition had already taken place on the site beyond Edinburgh Road, which also included Wolseley Road, Stone Street and Park Road, but the houses in the foreground seemingly took ages to finally be cleared. The Ringway sweeps from left to right of the picture. *(Neville Marsh)*

Wolseley Road, 24 April 1984. The derelict and desolate site prior to the construction of Park Mall shopping centre looking towards the business premises of Folkestone Glass (left) at the corner of Park Street and Park Road, and St Georges Square where the First World War tank is situated. The New China City Restaurant at the corner of St Georges Square and Park Road had been demolished for the shopping centre by this date. *(Neville Marsh)*

Edinburgh Road, 24 April 1984. The huge expanse of the Park Mall shopping development site, seen from the roof of the multi-storey car park. *(Neville Marsh)*

New Street, 6 July 1985. Demolition has taken place in New Street to make way for a new re-routed Edinburgh Road, which now starts at Park Street and finishes here at New Street. Nos 16a–18d New Street, which consisted of shops and business premises, had previously stood on this site which is situated behind the Old Prince of Wales public house. *(Neville Marsh)*

New Street, 6 July 1985. The New Street site adjacent to the infamous Ringway showing the excavations for the new re-routed Edinburgh Road. *(Neville Marsh)*

Edinburgh Road, 6 July 1985. The rest of the site had been cleared between New Street and Edinburgh Road in this view showing Park Street on the left and Castle Street (top left). *(Neville Marsh)*

Edinburgh Road, 6 July 1985. An entrance is being created to the shopping centre from the High Street (centre left) by demolishing the former International supermarket at nos 92–94 High Street. It had closed a few years earlier in 1980. The rear of the former Woolworths store can be seen to the left of the former International at nos 82–86. *(Neville Marsh)*

Edinburgh Road, 22 October 1985. The re-routed Edinburgh Road is seen here, being built between the Ringway and the new shopping centre site. The new road's primary use was not only to serve the car parks above what was then Sainsbury's and the new car park, but also to service the rear of the shops in the Upper High Street. *(Neville Marsh)*

Park Mall, September 1987. The newly opened Park Mall shortly after its completion. Some of the development's early tenants included Top Man/Top Shop, Jean Jeannie, ladieswear, Share Drugstore and NSS newsagents. The shopping centre is now owned by Ashford Borough Council. *(Steve Salter Archive)*

Ashford station, 1961. Much modernity came to Britain's railways during the 1960s. The post-electrification era saw various modernisation plans for stations, such as upgrading the facilities and infrastructure. The signage on the left suggests that modernisation at Ashford is taking place at the time of this photograph. During the 1960s, many stations across the South East's railway network were redeveloped or modernised. In Ashford's case, the original station, which opened in November 1842 and was extended in 1865, was subsequently demolished and replaced by a new station and bridge over the railway. Construction giant Mowlem built the new station which was completed by 1963. *(Steve Salter Archive)*

Ashford station, 1961. In the foreground, a new bridge is being built over the railway at Station Road, but the old traditional station premises are still standing. The town's current domestic station is situated where the rows of carriages are sitting on the left. *(Steve Salter Archive)*

Ashford station, 1961. Work appears to have commenced on the modernisation of Ashford station in this view which shows platform 1. Today, the Ashford International terminal covers the land seen here occupied by the old railway outbuildings. The cinema in Beaver Road can be seen on the far left, with the Victoria Hotel (centre left) in the background. *(Steve Salter Archive)*

Ashford station, 1962. A new wider and more modern bridge is seen here during the initial stages of its construction alongside the original tunnelled bridge that had stood for generations. Even this new bridge, built in 1962, was demolished due to alterations necessary to accommodate the Eurostar service. It utilises the power supply by deploying overhead pantographs. *(Steve Salter Archive)*

Station Road/Ashford station, 1962. This view shows workmen putting in the necessary concrete reinforcements for the new road bridge. *(Steve Salter Archive)*

Ashford station, 1962. Some of the traditional station buildings have already been demolished here in this view showing platforms 6 (centre left) and 5 (right). The lighting tower in the background is one of very few that survive today. *(Steve Salter Archive)*

Ashford station, 1962. The beautiful brick-built station buildings have disappeared. In the months that followed, a new overbridge booking hall was built parallel with the new road bridge. The stairwells and steel work are already in place here. *(Steve Salter Archive)*

Ashford station, 1962. The new stairs and steelwork on platform 2 at Ashford station. *(Steve Salter Archive)*

Ashford station, 1963. The smart new station platforms, prior to the construction of the new booking hall over the railway. *(Steve Salter Archive)*

Kennington Road, 1978. This stunning aerial view shows the William Harvey Hospital in Kennington Road, Willesborough. The site has been heavily extended in the years that have passed. *(Reflections/Weavers)*

Kennington Road, 1978. The multimillion-pound hospital built at Lacton Green, which replaced services at the nearby Willesborough Hospital in Kennington Road and Ashford Hospital in Kings Avenue. *(Reflections/Weavers)*

Kennington Road, 1978. A rare view showing the colossal site of the William Harvey Hospital during its construction, which took place between 1972 and 1978. This view shows the ramp and roadway to the outpatients department. Since it opened, the hospital has been progressively extended and upgraded. *(Steve Salter Archive)*

ACKNOWLEDGEMENTS

Over the years many local people and companies have been extremely kind and patient in assisting me with my research. Many have given me very valuable information, which has enabled me to put together an interesting record of the history of Ashford and to build up a substantial photographic collection.

I am overwhelmed by the continued support for and enormous success of *Changing Ashford*, *Ashford Then and Now*, *Ashford 1950–1980*, *Around Ashford*, *Remembering Ashford*, *Ashford Then and Now Revisited*, *Ashford in the 1960s and '70s* and *Ashford – A Rare Insight*. I am also very grateful to those who have followed my fortunes over the past 33 years. Without their kindness, this book wouldn't have been possible. As always, I have received much generosity from several individuals and organisations that have readily allowed me to use their pictures. I would therefore like to give heartfelt thanks to the following:

James Adams; the late Richard Filmer; Sue Cowan; Edwin Bartlett; Vasoulla and David Sims; Sylvia and Sid Marsh; Neville Marsh; the late Peter Goodwin; Mrs Pam Goodwin; David Worsley; Geoff Mathews; Sam Mathews; Jim Ashby and Mrs Joan Ashby; June at Ashford Gateway Plus (Library); Alastair Irvine, Robert Barman, Aidan Barlow, Mandy Curtin and all at the Kent Messenger Group; Pam Herrapath at Ashford Borough Council; Roger Lindfield; Bryan Badham; Allen and Mrs Christine Wells; Palma and Frankie Laughton; Jo-an Baxter; Rita Deverill and Mervyn Sperring; Bob and Daphne Davidson; Dukelease Properties; Owen Holmes; David Easton; Lindsay White; Richard Stafford; John Kennedy, architect; Terry and Eunice Burch; Katherine Burch; Nigel Gould; Karin Crittenden; Jessie Foster; Edith Neilson; Steve Godden; Steve Rabson; Les Freathy; David and Jean Emmett; Susan Jordan; Neil Jordan; Paul Jordan; Anne-Marie and Simon South; Trevor Cook.

Sadly, my good friend of 34 years, the celebrated historian, author and writer Richard Filmer, lost his battle with cancer in May 2017. Richard was one of the kindest and most generous people I knew. His passing is a huge loss to the town. He had a wealth of knowledge on his specialist subjects – of which there were too many to mention – and he served 54 years as a much-respected estate agent in the town. One of the subjects in which Richard was an acknowledged authority was the history of Ashford. It was through Richard's support and encouragement, as well as his unstinting generosity, that I write today. I knew Richard from the age of 10 and I miss him so very much. He who was an absolute gentleman with a wonderful sense of humour.

I was equally saddened to learn of the passing of another friend and absolute gem at the end of May; Peter Goodwin of Willesborough, whom I met through the Ashford Camcorder Club. We shared a mutual interest in photography and film-making. He was a kind and genuinely lovely man who could always lift your spirits by his chirpy tone and cheerful disposition. This book is for you, Richard and Peter.

I would finally like to express a special thanks to my special friend James for taking me under his wing and looking after me through challenging times with my mum who has vascular dementia.

Thanks are also due to anyone whose name has not been acknowledged here, either through an oversight or because the original source or present ownership of pictures is unknown or unavailable.

Many thanks to Matt Falcus at Destinworld Publishing for having faith in me and to my long-standing and fantastic editor Michelle Tilling; I am very grateful to you both for helping me to produce yet another successful book!